Rainbow of grace

Rainbow of grace

Learning from the life of Noah

Peter Jeffery

 EVANGELICAL PRESS

EVANGELICAL PRESS
Faverdale North Industrial Estate, Darlington, Co. Durham,
DL3 OPH, England

© Evangelical Press 1998
First published 1998

British Library Cataloguing in Publication Data available

ISBN O 852 34 4198

Printed in Great Britain by:
Rexam
Cardiff Road
Reading
Berks
RG1 8EX

Contents

17/7/10

<u>Heb 11:1</u> NLT

Faith — is the confidence that what
we hope for will actually
happen; it gives us assurance
about things we cannot see

1.
Noah's God

Every good thing Noah did was in response to either a command or action of God, and it is impossible to understand Noah apart from his relationship to God. This, of course, should be true of every believer. The person who lives by faith does so because he has come to know the God in whom his faith rests and therefore regards it as perfectly normal to trust and obey his God. Faith is not speculative uncertainty but a God-given trust in a great and sovereign Creator — it is the spiritual eyesight (Heb. 11:1). This does not make faith easy as is clearly illustrated in what God called Noah to do. In discussing the quality of Noah's faith John MacArthur said, 'He trusted absolutely as he pursued a task that seemed utterly foolish and useless from a human perspective. Imagine instantly surrendering all your time and effort to devote 120 years of building something you'd never seen (a vessel the size of an ocean liner or battleship) to protect you from something you'd never experienced (rain and flooding). Yet Noah did it without question. Noah's faith is unique in the sheer magnitude and time span of its assignment.'[1]

Noah's action would have been impossible without two things. First, his experience of God had to be real, and second, his understanding of the being of God had to match the actual character and power of God. Biblical faith is not blind! It gets its sight from seeing the glory and majesty of the almighty God. Today, many Christians whose experience of God is real in that they are truly regenerated fail to live a life of faith because their understanding of God is all wrong. A. W. Pink makes the point that the god of this twentieth century no more resembles the Supreme Sovereign of Holy Writ than the dim flickering of a candle resembles the glory of the midday sun. [2]

God complains in Psalm 50:21: 'You thought I was altogether like you'; in other words, we tend to think of God as merely a reflection of ourselves. We then think of God in terms of our own limitations. Thus the almighty God of Scripture is reduced to manageable terms, and Christianity is emptied of its very uniqueness, namely the supernatural power of God. There is only one way to escape this snare and that is to centre our thoughts upon what God has chosen to reveal to us about himself in Scripture.

Noah had nothing like the extent of biblical revelation that we have. His story comes after only a few pages have turned in the biblical record, yet even at that stage there has already been revealed a remarkable picture of God. It is far from the full truth that comes as Scripture unfolds but the essential truths are already all there. It is upon this knowledge and understanding of who God is, that Noah responds as he does to some amazing instructions.

In the first few chapters in Genesis God is revealed as the creator God, the holy God and the God of grace. These are the basic and essential truths about God that the rest of the Bible builds on as it reveals God to us.

The creator God

'In the beginning God created the heavens and the earth' (Gen. 1:1) are not only the first words in the Bible, but they also tell us the first and most basic truth about God. He precedes everything and everyone. Apart from God there would be no universe. It is not the intention of this book to explore the creation versus evolution argument, as many fine books deal with this better than this writer can. Our purpose is to see Noah's God. As far as Noah was concerned God created the world. He would have thought it incredible that anyone could believe the theory of evolution, not because he did not have the scientific knowledge we have today, but because he had a spiritual knowledge of God that sadly few seem to possess in our society. Noah believed in a supernatural God who could do supernatural things. He also believed that since God was the Creator this gave him certain rights in the lives of men and women. Man's duty to the Creator was to obey his commands (Gen. 6:22; 7:5).

These two beliefs of Noah are firmly rejected by people today and perhaps this is why folk are so ready to reject creation and accept evolution. If we reject creation we will almost certainly reject the supernatural activity of God and then everything in life becomes a matter of chance. 'Eat, drink and be merry for tomorrow we die' will then be a reasonable philosophy to live by. Furthermore, people do not like the idea of a God who has rights in our lives and can make demands upon us. They want a comfortable God who can be manipulated, a sort of cosy Santa Claus who only exists for their convenience. But the God of the Bible is not like this.

Thus people either reject Christianity altogether or so water down the truth about the God they say they believe in, that it becomes meaningless.

They would react in horror to the idea that God has every right to do with his creation what he likes, even deciding to destroy the world. They would say that God has no right to do that; that is immoral and barbaric; and suggest that that could not be the God of the New Testament. Or because their god is so small they would doubt that he had the power to flood the earth. If Noah had reacted in either of these ways he would not have taken the word of God seriously and he would not have built the ark. It was fundamentally his understanding of who God is in relation to man that caused him to take the warning of judgement very seriously and left him in no doubt that God was able to carry out the threat.

Everything in the Christian life is governed by our concept of God. Wishy-washy, half thought out, semi-biblical views about God have greatly impoverished Christianity. To believe in the creator God who has power and rights is not a matter of science, but of effective and certain faith. Why seek to live a holy life if we do not believe God is concerned about sin? Why evangelize if God has no power to save sinners today? Pathetic fatalism has replaced a vibrant faith in many Christians and the only answer to that is to once again see the true, holy, majestic and sovereign God of Scripture.

The men and women that God uses are, like Noah, people of faith. 'By faith Noah, when warned about things not yet seen, in holy fear built an ark to save his family' (Heb. 11:7). We need to capture again an understanding of the greatness and power of our God. He is Creator because he is sovereign. By the sovereignty of God we mean the absolute rule of God and his authority over all creation: God can do what he likes, when he likes and with whom he likes, not as a fickle or despotic ruler, but as the absolute sovereign over all his creation. This is a rule which covers everything without exception — creation, animals, weather and man. God is sovereign because he is God. He is not like us, cumbered about with all sorts of limitations and restrictions (Rom. 9:20-21). Any understanding of God that limits his sovereignty will seriously hamper our usefulness in his service. Martin Luther once accused the great Bible scholar Erasmus, 'Your thoughts of God are too human.' And that was one reason why Erasmus was never any more than a great scholar while Luther, with his eye on the sovereign God, was used to set the world ablaze through the Reformation.

The holy God

Holiness is the attribute of God which the Bible emphasizes more than any other. It means an entire freedom from all moral evil and an absolute moral perfection. The result of this is God's hatred of all sin and his total intolerance of it in his creation (do not confuse God's intolerance with his longsuffering — all sin will be punished, though God tolerates it so that the elect might be saved — 1 Peter 3:20). In creating man, God made him in his own image, in his likeness (Gen. 1:26). Man was made both sinless and holy for it was only in this state that he could really enjoy God and please his Creator. Sin robbed man of what he was created for and creation of its perfection — it was no longer 'good' (Rom. 8:22).

11

Divine holiness reacted against sin as Adam and Eve were banished from the Garden of Eden. Cain was warned of the danger of sin as God describes it as being like a wild animal crouching at Cain's door ready to pounce upon him and master him (Gen. 4:7). The very fact that God issues this warning shows us that he is still concerned about his wayward creation and he has not given up on man. But still he will not tolerate sin. By the time we get to Genesis 6 it is as if God has had enough: 'The Lord saw how great man's wickedness on the earth had become, and that every inclination of the thoughts of his heart was only evil all the time. The Lord was grieved that he had made man on the earth, and his heart was filled with pain. So the Lord said, "I will wipe mankind, whom I have created, from the face of the earth — men and animals, and creatures that move along the ground, and birds of the air — for I am grieved that I have made them"' (Gen. 6:5-7).

Sin not only grieves God but it fills his heart with pain. It is not that God is a killjoy and does not like to see man enjoying himself, nor that God is too sensitive and ought to give and take a little. God is holy and our sin is an attack upon that holiness. We cannot understand holiness because we have never experienced it ourselves nor seen it in others. It is a concept beyond our grasp and consequently God's holiness is something we cannot even imagine. We can tolerate sin, and are prone to admire it and enjoy it. It rarely grieves us or brings pain to our hearts unless its consequences mar our life with personal inconvenience or suffering. We are born in the sin that surrounds us in this world. Even after we are saved we still battle with sin, as it still stands ready to pounce on us and master us as it did Cain. Sometimes it is violent and evil, sometimes pleasant and attractive, but it is always opposed to God and God is always opposed to it.

God's wrath is an inevitable product of his holiness. The Flood, which was the evidence of the awful wrath of God, was also the evidence that the God we have to deal with is a holy God.

The God of grace

Man was created sinless. He was put into a sinless paradise and everything he could possibly need was provided for him in abundance, yet in that situation man sinned. He was not deprived or badly treated, he was not in need or desperate for nourishment. He had no grounds to plead for forgiveness and a second chance. His sin has opened an unbridgeable gap between him and his Creator. His sin has pained the heart of the very one who gave him his life. Because of sin he is in this world without God and without hope. He deserves all that he gets!

God's holiness is man's greatest problem because it leaves him alone with his sin in the presence of an angry God. But there is more to God than simply holiness. He is also gracious and loving, and this alone gives the sinner hope. Grace is the free, unmerited gift of God to a people who not only do not deserve it, but who deserve the opposite. It is God showing goodness to a people who deserve judgement. God shows mercy because he is God and for no other reason outside of his divine character. He is not only sovereign in condemning the world because of its sin, but also in having mercy on whom he will have mercy, and having compassion on whomever he will have compassion (Rom. 9:15).

13

Rainbow of grace

In Genesis 3:15 we are given the first hint in Scripture of the grace of God: 'And I will put enmity between you and the woman, and between your offspring and hers; he will crush your head, and you will strike his heel.' Commenting on this verse E. J. Young writes, 'In the Old Testament there is a remarkable progression in God's revelation of the truth concerning the Messiah. As we turn over the pages of the Old Testament, examining one after another of the Messianic prophecies, we are struck by the strange manner in which God progressively reveals more and more concerning the Person of the One whom he is to send into the world to heal the breach between himself and the fallen human race. In Genesis, as we proceed from prophecy to prophecy, we do learn that salvation is to be through Abraham, and then furthermore we learn that it will be through Isaac rather than Ishmael. As we close the book of Genesis we have the knowledge that we are to look to the tribe of Judah for the coming Redeemer. Yet only dimly, as it were, do we see him. We do see him but not with the clear light of fulfilment that characterizes the pages of the New Testament.' [3]

Noah's ark is also a vivid symbol of divine grace. It was intended by God as an instrument of deliverance to preserve both human and animal life on earth. It was seen as such by the writer to the Hebrews: 'By faith Noah, when warned about things not yet seen, in holy fear built an ark to save his family' (Heb. 11:7). The ark showed that God had not finished with his creation and still cared for men and women in spite of their sinful rebellion. After the Flood (Gen. 8:9-17) God gave Noah an unusual sign of his grace. The rainbow was a thing of beauty and spoke to Noah of the continuing grace of a sovereign and holy creator God.

2.
Noah's world

The state of the world in Noah's day is stated graphically in Genesis 6:5: 'The Lord saw how great man's wickedness on the earth had become, and that every inclination of the thoughts of his heart was only evil all the time.' The words used are devastating, *every inclination ... only evil ... all the time.* There was no limit to the sin of these people and no let up in their rebellion against God. The warning about sin's ambition that God had given Cain is now clearly seen — sin had them totally in its grip.

Sin in the heart

When sin first revealed itself in human experience it seemed so harmless and unimportant. Eve merely picked a fruit from a tree and shared it with her husband. What could possibly be wrong with that? She wasn't stealing the fruit — it was her garden to care for. She wasn't selfishly keeping it for herself — she shared it with Adam.

It is true that the act itself was fairly innocuous but what was wrong with it was that God had very clearly forbidden it. With the command had come a dire warning so that they were aware of how serious the matter was: 'You must not eat from the tree of the knowledge of good and evil, for when you eat of it you will surely die' (Gen. 2:17). Adam and Eve chose to ignore both the command and the warning. They listened instead to the lies of Satan. The sin had already been committed in their thoughts and in their hearts before Eve's hand reached to pluck the fruit from the tree. Man's problem is that he always judges sin by the act and not the thought of the heart.

In Genesis 4, we have the story of Cain and Abel. No one would claim that Cain's murder of his brother was innocuous, but that act, like the sin of his parents, stemmed from a heart in rebellion against God. From man's point of view the actions of Eve and Cain do not bear comparison. It could be argued that one is trivial and the other serious. They may both have been wrong but surely you cannot equate them. It is like equating a boy stealing apples from the farmer's orchard with gangsters mowing down innocent bystanders in a bank raid. Technically both actions broke the law but the consequences of one were negligible and the other tragic. This argument sounds reasonable until you come back to Genesis. What were the consequences of Adam and Eve's sin? Paul tells us in Romans 5:12: 'just as sin entered the world through one man, and death through sin, and in this way death came to all men, because all sinned'. Dr Lloyd-Jones says, 'What is clear then is this, that Paul is saying here quite plainly that all sinned in Adam and that all are guilty before God on account of that one sin of Adam when he deliberately transgressed God's commandment. God has imputed to the whole of the human race, including ourselves, that one sin of Adam. Adam sinned, and we all sinned.' [1]

Man's law deals with human wrongdoing in various degrees of severity. It has no other way of dealing with sins. But God does not work like this. He is always concerned about the heart, because as Jesus said, 'For out of the heart come evil thoughts, murder, adultery, sexual immorality, theft, false testimony' (Matt. 15:19). And in the Old Testament the prophet Jeremiah wrote, 'The heart is deceitful above all things and beyond cure' (Jer. 17:9). God distinguishes between sin and sins. Sins are the wrong acts we do but they are the fruit of a heart that is polluted by sin. It is not our sins that make us sinners, but we sin because we are by nature sinners. Thus the human heart dominated by sin is the real problem. Man can only deal with the fruit of particular sins but God's aim is to deal with the root problem of sin. This is always the difference to man's approach to sin and God's — 'The Lord does not look at the things man looks at. Man looks at the outward appearance, but the Lord looks at the heart' (1 Sam. 16:7). Our whole being is saturated to its very core with the foul stench of sin. We are born in it, we live in it, and without Christ, we will die in it.

In 1991 a cardiologist told me that I had a serious heart condition and needed a quadruple bypass operation to deal with it. How did he know? First of all he was guided by the symptoms — pain, tightening of the chest, breathlessness and an inability to do ordinary things. There is so much heart disease today that many will recognize these symptoms, but

17

thankfully most people do not suffer in this way. But God says we all have a serious heart condition and in the Bible he tells us that the symptoms of this are our sins. Every human heart is spiritually exactly the same. This is why Paul says in Romans 3:10 and 12: 'There is no-one righteous, not even one ... there is no-one who does good, not even one.' We may be tempted to think that the Apostle is overstating his case, after all we know many good, kind, generous people. If he is exaggerating then so too is David because Paul is only quoting from Psalm 14. And if both these great men are wrong, then so too is Jesus because he said exactly the same thing in Mark 10:18: 'No-one is good'. Obviously Jesus, David and Paul are using the word good in a different sense than we do. When we look at ourselves in relation to others, we find that many perform kind acts and that some are better than others. However, when we compare ourselves to God, we soon also recognize that as a means of salvation none of us have a goodness that can satisfy God's demands. Once again it is a matter of outward actions and the inward condition of our hearts.

Commenting on Genesis 6:5-8, James Montgomery Boice writes, 'The first thing these verses tell us is that sin is an *internal* matter. That is, it is not merely a question of such outward acts as adultery, stealing, murder, and other crimes, but of the thoughts of the heart. Second, Genesis 6:5 tells us that sin is *pervasive*. That is, because it comes out of the heart, which controls what we think and do, sin necessarily affects every part of our being so that nothing we think, do, plan, or are, is unaffected by it. This is the main thrust of the verse. It says that "*every* inclination of the thoughts of (man's heart) was *only* evil all the time". We need to explain this carefully, of course. For when we say that men and women are "totally depraved" (a good theological term for "only evil all the time"), we do not mean to say that they never do anything that we would call good or that they never have aspirations in the direction of real good. We mean rather that even their best is always spoiled by their essentially sinful nature.'[2]

The wages of sin

Paul writes in Romans 6 that the wages of sin is death, and that is exactly what God says of Noah's contemporaries in Genesis 6, 'I will wipe mankind, whom I have created, from the face of the earth' (Gen. 6:7). God's response to sin is always absolute. It is either total forgiveness or total judgement.

Man is left in no doubt as to how God regards sin. Adam was told that if he ate from the tree of the knowledge of good and evil, he would die. The moment he disobeyed God and ate, he died spiritually. In other words his whole relationship to God changed as is very clear in Genesis 3:8-24. Physical death also became inevitable for him. It is true that he lived for 930 years but we read in Genesis 5:5: 'and then he died'. Chapter 5 is a remarkable chapter as we read of the amazing number of years these men lived. But the recurring and powerful phrase repeated time and time again in the chapter is, 'and then he died'. Death was the recurring inevitability in every man's life. We differ from them in the length of our days but we have this in common: it will one day be said of us, 'and then he died'. We have death in common because we have sin in common. The people of Noah's day lived a lot longer than people today, but like us they had to receive the wages of sin and they died.

Bala in North Wales is a very Welsh town. The language spoken in the homes and shops is Welsh, and the names on the houses are, with very few exceptions, Welsh. One of these exceptions is the nameplate on a house that is passed if you went into the town on the Dolgellau road. The name is *Pros Kairon*. It is not Welsh, but Greek, and means *for a while*. Whoever gave the name to the house had wisdom and understanding. He knew that no home is permanent in this world. The house may stand for a hundred years or more, but we are here only for a while.

No one, not even those in Genesis 5, is in this world for ever. Our sin brings death and judgement upon us. And it does not matter how death comes, it is always the wages of sin. The men in Genesis 5 died naturally and perhaps quietly, whereas those in Genesis 6 died violently in the Flood, but all were dying for one reason only — sin.

When my heart condition was diagnosed by the consultant, he told me that the only answer was surgery. My problem was a blockage of the arteries. This had to be dealt with to allow the blood to do its job of taking oxygen to my heart. Therefore I needed open-heart surgery. The problem had to be exposed before it could be dealt with. Our problem is sin. It pollutes the heart and makes us unacceptable to God. But even as God prepared salvation via the ark for Noah, so he has prepared a Saviour for us in the Lord Jesus Christ. The teaching of Romans 5 is that we are all 'in Adam' and therefore we all die, but those who are 'in Christ' are spared the judgement of death and receive grace and life. 'For if, by the trespass of the one man, death reigned through that one man, how much more will those who receive God's abundant provision of grace and of the gift of righteousness reign in life through the one man, Jesus Christ' (Rom. 5:17).

Even those who are Christians will die physically but the sting of death is removed for them by their Saviour. They do not die under judgement but under grace and the difference is glorious. John Wesley could say of the first Methodists, 'Our people die well.' This was true because they believed what the Scripture said about death. Richard Baxter, the Puritan, was asked on his deathbed, 'How are you?' His answer was, 'Almost well and almost home.'

3.
Noah's righteousness

In a world so rotten and evil that even God's 'heart was filled with pain' (Gen. 6:6), there stands one beacon of light. One man stands for God and against the sin of his contemporaries. This man, Noah, found grace (NIV: favour) in the eyes of the Lord. Noah was a righteous man but where did he get his righteousness from? He certainly did not receive it from the example of his friends and acquaintances. But his great-grandfather Enoch was a godly man and perhaps his influence came down through Methuselah and Lamech to Noah. It is clear from Genesis 5:28-29 ('When Lamech had lived 182 years, he had a son. He named him Noah and said, "He will comfort us in the labour and painful toil of our hands caused by the ground the Lord has cursed"') that Lamech thought in terms of the activity of God in men's lives. C. Leupold writes, 'By the spirit of prophecy Lamech, like other godly patriarchs, sensed that in an unusual way this one would bring comfort to the troubled race. In reality Noah did this by preserving the small godly remnant in the ark. This unusual form of the comfort Lamech may never have dreamed of. Yet his prophecy is a valid one.'[1] Boice makes the point that 'Noah was the last descendant in the godly line of Adam through Seth. By the time of the flood these ancestors had died, but like the righteous in all ages, their works lived after them — in this case in Noah, who had learned his lessons well.'[2]

So Noah, in spite of the world he lived in, had grown up in a home where faith in God was no stranger. This clearly is an important factor in understanding Noah because we should never minimize the effect of a godly upbringing in moulding a man's character. But it is equally as clear that this is not enough, because of Lamech's other sons and daughters (v. 30) who knew nothing of righteousness and perished in the Flood.

The answer to the question — where did Noah get his righteousness from? — is that he found it in the grace of God. Verse 8 of chapter 6 does not tell us that he earned or deserved grace but that he found it in God. Some folk think that Noah found grace and favour with God because he was righteous and lived a blameless life. That is to put verse 9 before verse 8 as if one is the consequence of the other, but Boice says, 'Noah's righteousness was the product of his having found favour and is therefore the proof of that favour, not its ground. This is a great biblical principle, namely, that the grace of God always comes before any thing. We imagine in our unsanctified state that God loves us for what we are intrinsically or for what we have done or can become. But God does not love us because of that, nor is he gracious to us because of that. On the contrary, he loves us solely because he loves us. He is gracious to us only because he is.'[3]

In all his dealings with man God always takes the initiative. His actions always precede ours. This is stated in the Old Testament in Deuteronomy 7:7-8: 'The Lord did not set his affection on you and choose you because you were more numerous than other peoples, for you were the fewest of all peoples. But it was because the Lord loved you and kept the oath he swore to your forefathers that he brought you out with a mighty hand and redeemed you from the land of slavery', and in the New Testament in 1 John 4:10: 'This is love: not that we loved God, but that he loved us and sent his Son as an atoning sacrifice for our sins.' If grace depended upon anything in us it would not be grace. Grace is God's free unmerited favour to sinners who do not deserve it and in fact deserve his wrath and judgement.

When Noah found grace his life was changed. Three things in particular about this man were brought about by the grace of God. He was righteous in his standing before God. He was blameless in his relationship to the world. And in his spiritual and moral life, Noah walked with God.

Noah was righteous

In the Bible when a man is described as righteous it can refer either to his standing before the holy God in that he is just and acceptable to God, or it can refer to the quality of his life in that he is living a sanctified and holy life. Of course, if the first is true then the second should be the fruit of it because grace leads to a sanctified life. Genesis 6 goes on to tell us that not only was Noah righteous but he was also blameless among the people of his time, therefore it would be reasonable to assume that 'righteous' here refers to his standing before God.

Noah was exactly like the other people described in Genesis 6:5 in that he was 'in Adam' and therefore had a fallen and corrupt human nature. He too was under the wrath and condemnation of the holy God. All men and women are born in this condition, that is why Paul says there is no one who is righteous (Rom. 3:10). To be human and to be righteous is an impossibility apart from the grace of God. It is grace that made Noah what he was.

Grace exists, and is necessary, for two reasons: the character of man and the character of God. Though man was created in the image of God, able to know and enjoy him, when man sinned he became separated from God, and sin has since dominated all his actions. He is now an alien to God his Creator, and because of his sinful character he can do nothing about it. God's character, on the other hand, is such that he cannot condone or overlook sin. His holiness, truth and justice demand that man must be dealt with and sin must be punished. These two factors, taken on their own, would condemn all men to an eternity in hell. But God's character is also such that though he hates sin yet he loves the guilty sinner who deserves his judgement. Divine love therefore plans salvation, and divine grace provides salvation. Grace is necessary because without it sinful man has no hope;

and grace is possible because of the loving and merciful character of God. Once this truth is grasped and understood, grace becomes the most thrilling thing there is.

Grace and righteousness belong together as cause and effect. Grace is the cause of salvation. The gospel centres upon the great doctrine of justification by faith. It is in justification that we receive pardon for sin and peace with God, and justification is the product of divine grace (Rom. 3:24). Grace flows from the tender heart of God the Father, and it is embodied in Jesus Christ the Son of God. It is Jesus who makes grace a reality by fulfilling the demands of God's righteousness. He dies the just for the unjust; he appeases the holy wrath of God; he sheds his blood to cover our sin, and he takes our sin away (Rom. 3:25-26; 5:9; Col. 1:20). All this is because of grace.

The guilty sinner is only acceptable to God because of what the Lord Jesus Christ has done for him. The Bible teaches justification by faith alone, and justification is the sovereign work of God whereby he declares the guilty sinner to be righteous and the rightful demands of the law satisfied (Rom. 8:3-4). Noah, like every other child of God before or since Christ, was only acceptable to God because of the merit of the Lord Jesus Christ. This is why Hebrews 11, speaking of Noah and the other Old Testament saints, says, 'These were all commended for their faith, yet none of them received what had been promised. God had planned something better for us so that only together with us would they be made perfect' (vv. 39-40). And the author and perfecter of their and our faith is Jesus (Heb. 12:2).

Noah was blameless

Noah was a solitary saint among a people totally corrupted by the vileness of sin. Today Christians often find it difficult to live a godly life if they are the only believer in the family, or the class, or the workplace. But Noah appeared to have no fellowship at all because the Scripture tells us nothing of the spiritual quality of his wife and children. He certainly had no church and no ministry to feed his soul. Perhaps it was his solitariness that was his strength because he had no one but the Lord to depend on. One of our problems is that we can become too dependent upon other believers. Fellowship with other saints is a blessed gift of God and it is not to be neglected, but it is no substitute for fellowship with God himself. Just as some believers go from conference to conference to get a spiritual lift, so others live their whole devotional life within the confines of the four walls of their place of worship. Outside these walls they never pray and never open the Bible, consequently their life is not marked by blamelessness but by compromise and worldliness. We cannot live the Christian life by proxy. We need a living and vibrant relationship with the Lord. It is not good to be without fellowship and ministry but sometimes it is forced upon us by circumstances. The life of Noah shows us that such solitariness need not be a spiritual disaster but can be a blessing if it deepens the reality of God to us.

Noah could have no fellowship with men and women of whom every inclination of the thoughts of their hearts was evil all the time, but he did have an influence upon them. He lived a life that was blameless and this did two things. It condemned the world (Heb. 11:7), in that it left people without any excuse. Noah showed that sin was not inevitable and godliness was not impossible. If one man could live to the glory of God so too could others. Secondly, he lived his life in 'godly fear' (Heb. 11:7). It must have become obvious to his neighbours that Noah was different from them not because he was awkward or unsociable but because he was motivated by a genuine holy fear of God. They may have thought that building an ark was ridiculous but they could not dismiss Noah as a crank. There is something powerfully compulsive about a man living in holy fear and godly awe. It invokes a silent admiration and a sad envy in many an unbeliever's heart.

Noah was blameless, not because he was without sin, but because of his relationship to God. His faith was in the One who would one day send the Redeemer who would redeem him and present him without fault to the Father (Jude 24). A blameless life, if it is motivated by godly fear, is a powerful weapon in God's hand. Whatever people thought of Noah they could not dismiss him or ignore him. His blameless life was making an impact long before the first plank was cut and shaped for the ark.

Noah walked with God

Of only two men is it said in Scripture that they walked with God. One is Noah and the other is his great-grandfather Enoch

(Gen. 5:22). It is a phrase used to describe an especially close relationship with God. The mind and the heart are taken up with God, communion is habitual and deep, and the divine presence is not a doctrinal concept or an inexperienced longing, but the norm. God is real. God is near. God is the all-consuming passion of the life.

The three phrases, Noah was righteous, he was blameless and he walked with God, are all interdependent. If righteousness makes fellowship with the world impossible, then sin makes fellowship with God impossible. Two cannot walk together unless there is an agreement between them to do so (Amos 3:3). So not only did Noah walk with God but God was pleased to walk with this man. God looked at a life that was not sinless but none the less shone out in a dark world.

4.
Noah's faith

When Noah found grace in the eyes of the Lord he received from God the gift of faith. Grace always leads to faith so Hebrews 11:7 tells us that Noah's actions in building the ark were all done by faith. God's grace was the motivating cause but Noah's faith led him to cut and shape the wood and nail the planks to construct the ark. Without the grace of God there would have been no ark, but Noah did not wake up one morning and see the finished ark in his back garden. It is amazing to think that God uses human agents in carrying out his plans.

God told Noah what wood to use and gave him the exact dimensions but Noah had to build it. 'Noah did everything just as God commanded him' (Gen. 6:22). He did so because he believed God's warning of coming judgement and he believed that the ark was God's provision of mercy for himself and his family. He believed God — not the vague feeling that something might happen, but Noah possessed an unshakeable certainty of the reality of the message. That is what faith is. It was not Noah's faith that saved him from the Flood any more than it is our faith that saves us from the judgement of God upon our sin. Grace saves, not faith. But grace comes to us through the channel of faith. In salvation faith is an unwavering trust in the Lord Jesus Christ as the only Saviour to deal with sin. It is not merely an intellectual assent to a set of doctrines, but a coming to Christ in repentance, crying for mercy. Faith hears the truth of the gospel, believes it and then acts upon it. Saving faith progresses from an intellectual acceptance of certain facts to a real trusting in Christ and what he has done on our behalf and for our salvation. Faith is a response of the mind and the heart to the Saviour of whom the gospel speaks.

It was the same with Noah. A. W. Pink says, 'If Noah had not prepared an ark in obedience to God's command, would he not have perished in the flood? Then was it his own efforts which prevented him from death in the great deluge? No indeed, it was the preserving power of God. That ark had neither mast, sail, nor steering wheel; only the gracious hand of the Lord kept that frail barque from being splintered to atoms on the rocks and mountains. Then what is the relation between these two things? This; Noah made use of the *means* which God had prescribed, and by His grace and power those means were made effectual unto his preservation ... salvation by grace alone does not exclude the imperative necessity of our using the means which God has appointed and prescribed.' [1]

Real faith

To appreciate Noah's faith we must see him in the context of his day and age. He lived in a world of uncontrolled sin. Everywhere he looked, sin was flaunting itself. He was not sinless himself but the behaviour of all those around him must have grieved his heart. When God said he was going to destroy all these people, he accepts that as God's right and as morally correct. He did not plead for the people as Abraham did for Sodom and Gomorrah. He knew there were no righteous people so he could not use Abraham's plea that if there were fifty or forty or twenty or ten righteous men that God would hold back his judgement. He was asked to build a boat so large that there was no possibility of ever getting it to the sea. He was given the immense task of gathering the male and female of every living creature. He was told that God was going to send rain for forty days and nights, but at that time there had never been any rain. The earth was watered by a mist (Gen. 2:6, NKJV). To do all this would inevitably bring upon him the ridicule and criticism of others, but he did it. For a hundred and twenty years he did it and he did it by faith.

Jesus referred to Noah's day when he said, 'For in the days before the flood, people were eating and drinking, marrying and giving in marriage, up to the day Noah entered the ark' (Matt. 24:38). Everything was going on as usual except for Noah and his ark. The outworking of his faith made Noah look like an oddity, as he was preoccupied with doing the will of God. If we have a real faith in God it should have the same effect upon us in our day and age. The only way a Christian can be at home in this world is by living a life of compromise. Worldliness is the outward evidence of a heart that has compromised and a faith that is shallow. There is nothing wrong in the things Jesus refers to in Matthew 24:38. They only become wrong for the believer when they become the all-consuming passion of his life and when God is fitted in around them.

Noah's faith led him to take God seriously. Does your faith do the same or are you merely playing at Christianity? Is God a hobby not the all-consuming passion of your life? If we took the warnings in Scripture of judgement and hell seriously, we would evangelize more urgently. If we were as concerned about God's opinion of us as we are of our friends, our lives would be more like Noah's.

The man of faith always takes God seriously. He has no alternative because his faith is a product of grace, and grace has taught him the reality of God's judgement upon his sin and the wonder of God's salvation for repentant sinners.

Holy faith

'By faith Noah, when warned about things not yet seen, in holy fear built an ark to save his family' (Heb. 11:7). The faith which causes a man to take God seriously will also produce in him a holy fear and reverential awe of God. This is not the fear of terror but of respect, wonder, amazement, astonishment at the being and character of God. And this fear is a strong impetus to action in obeying the Lord's commandments. This holy fear is markedly absent from the lives of many Christians today and is one of the main reasons for the shallow and insipid faith that breeds worldliness and lack of commitment to the work of the gospel.

Why is it that in most evangelical churches it is so difficult to get believers to attend the prayer meeting? Is it not that we have lost the sense of awe and wonder at being in the presence of God? When the fear of God goes, so too does the awareness of the sheer privilege of prayer. We believe we can build the ark without God's instructions. We do it our way, without prayer, and the result is many of the monstrosities that have cluttered up evangelicalism in the past fifty years.

Why is it that evangelicals have no sense of urgency about evangelism? It is true that we get stirred up every ten years or so when the 'big event' comes to town, but day in and day out little is done to reach people with the gospel. Why is it that believing parents seem more concerned that their teenage children get good academic results at school than that they are saved? Once we stop taking God seriously the biblical warnings of judgement and hell get watered down. If we believe what God says about judgement then those of our family and friends without Christ are going to hell. A holy fear is the greatest impetus to biblical evangelism.

Why is it that so many evangelical churches are struggling financially and seem content to keep their pastors on scandalously low salaries? Once again we come back to a lack of holy fear in the members. Christians will happily spend more on a meal out than they will give to the work of the gospel. This attitude affects not only our giving but also our attendance and commitment to the church.

If we want to be effective Christians in doing the will of God then we need to follow Noah's example. Faith and fear are an invincible combination in promoting the work of God. But to some people faith in God and fear of God are a contradiction. These folk major on the love of God almost to the denial of the effective holiness of God. They therefore have all sorts of problems with the stories of Uzzah and the Ark of the Covenant (2 Samuel 6), and with Ananias and Sapphira (Acts 5). They argue the God of love would never do such things. Gordon Keddie answers such objections: 'God knew Uzzah's heart and the (to us) sudden application of his judgement only proves how little we see of the true provocation of human sin. The case of Ananias and Sapphira is very similar, with respect to summary judgement for something that looks outwardly trivial to us but was, in fact, inwardly the deepest contempt for God. This judgement, too, was designed to awaken the people to a realization that God is never to be trifled with (Acts 5:1-11). Secondly, God is to be accorded all reverence and holy fear (Ps. 89:7). The goodness and severity of God are co-ordinate, not contradictory truths. His severity with Uzzah is a measure of Uzzah's violation of his standard of goodness. God cannot trample on his own holiness and he will not allow others to do that with impunity. In the last analysis, this is what true justice is: God's perfect vindication of absolutely everything that is holy by means of his perfect retributive judgement upon all that is opposed to his sovereignty and righteousness. This is, of course, why the atoning death of Christ is necessary for sinners to be saved. Uzzah's death reminds us of the issues of life and death, concerning both time and eternity, and calls us to bow in humble submission before the Lord.'[2]

5.
Noah's ark and the Flood

To most people the story of Noah's ark is an interesting and unusual story for children but certainly not one to be taken seriously by adults. It is to them another Bible myth with little or no resemblance to reality. This line of reasoning is understandable if one ignores one crucial factor in the story. That factor is God. If God is taken out then no one could be expected to believe it happened. But the whole story of Noah's ark centres around the activity of God and with God nothing is impossible.

Today, God is a strange concept to most folk. They cannot think in terms of an almighty being even if they have a nominal belief in God. Without God any Bible story that involves the supernatural activity of God, things like the virgin birth and the miracles, makes no sense at all. Biblical Christianity both in its historical narratives and its doctrinal truths acknowledges a God who can do what the mind of man cannot even imagine.

The ark is not really Noah's at all, it is God's. God conceived the idea and planned its design, Noah was only the labourer working to very specific plans. The purpose of the ark was God's and when it was built he was the one who shut the door on Noah and his family (Gen. 7:16).

Credible

Is this story credible or are the details given in Genesis just too unbelievable? Most people ignore the details and dismiss the story without any serious attempt to answer the question of credibility. If you see a picture of Noah's ark in a children's picture book it is usually depicted as a small boat with two pointy ends, a little house on the deck and a giraffe's neck sticking out of the chimney pot. The picture shouts at you that the story is ridiculous and not to be taken seriously. But how different is the real ark put before us in Genesis.

The ark was 450 feet (140 m.) long, 75 feet (23 m.) wide and 45 feet (14 m.) high (Gen. 6:15). It was very much like a modern barge, designed more to float than to sail. It was huge; in fact it was not until 1858 that a vessel of greater length was built. At 450 feet it was a little under the length of one and a half football pitches. In simulated tests in water it was found that a box-like structure of the ark's dimensions was exceedingly stable, indeed, almost impossible to capsize. Whatever our judgement about the carrying capacity of the ark, therefore, there is an obvious presumption in favour of the design having come from God. For how would Noah or anyone else at that time know how to construct such a large seaworthy craft except by revelation?

From the point of view of its design and stability it was credible, but what about its ability to hold all those animals? John Whitcomb tells us that the ark 'was a barge, not a ship with sloping sides, and therefore had one-third more carrying capacity than a ship of similar dimensions. Assuming the minimum length of the cubit (18 inches or 0.5 m), the ark had a capacity of nearly 1,400,000 cubic feet, and was therefore so huge that 522 modern railroad box cars could be fitted inside. And since two each of all air-breathing creatures in the world today could be comfortably carried in only 150 box cars, there was plenty of room in Noah's ark for all the kinds alive today, plus two each of extinct air-breathing types, plus food for them all.' [1]

The ark was not designed to sail or be navigated anywhere, its purpose was to float and to provide for Noah and his family a place of safety when God's judgement fell upon the earth.

Mount Ararat

Genesis 8:4 tells us that after the Flood the ark came to rest on Mount Ararat. This is a mountain in northern Turkey near the Russian border. It is nearly 17,000 feet high and today the top 4000 feet are covered with an ice-cap up to 800 feet deep.

Christians have always been intrigued to discover if part of the ark still exists upon Ararat. Josephus, the Jewish historian, writing about A.D. 37 says, 'All the writers of barbarian histories make mention of this flood and this ark; among whom is Berosus the Chaldean; for when he is describing the circumstances of the flood, he goes on thus; — it is said there is still some part of this ship in Armenia, at the mountain of the Cordyacans; and that some people carry off pieces of the bitumen, which they take away, and use chiefly as amulets for the averting of mischiefs.' [2] Since then there have been many claims of possible sightings of the ark but no definite proof. This goes right up to the present time when it was claimed on BBC radio in 1997 that the CIA had pictures taken from a spy plane over Ararat which reveal an object that could well be the ark. A curiosity about Ararat is interesting but it is no more than that. If the ark was discovered on the mountain, what would it prove? It would prove that *the flood probably did take place*. But Christians know that anyway from the testimony of Scripture. It may cause some unbelievers to think again but it would not lead to the salvation of one lost soul. Salvation is by grace through faith not by archaeological evidence or any other physical evidence. Jesus tells us this in Luke 16:27-31 in the story of the rich man and Lazarus. The rich man in hell cries out, '"Then I beg you, father, send Lazarus to my father's house, for I have five brothers. Let him warn them, so that they will not also come to this place of torment." Abraham replied, "They have Moses and the Prophets; let them listen to them." "No, father Abraham," he said, "but if someone from the dead goes to them, they will repent." He said to him, "If they do not listen to Moses and the Prophets, they will not be convinced even if someone rises from the dead."'

Obviously the more factual proof that is accumulated, the better. But in their desire to prove the truth of Scripture to unbelievers Christians can become gullible and grasp at any straw. For instance in the 1970s an article appeared in many evangelical magazines called 'Space Scientists' Discovery'. The articles started in this way, 'One of the most amazing things happened recently to our astronauts and space scientists at Green Belt Maryland; they were checking the position of the sun, moon and planets in space and where they would be 100 years and 1000 years from now. We have to know this orbit. We have to lay out the orbit in terms of the life of the satellite and where the planets will be so that the whole thing will not bog down. They ran the computer measurements back and forth over the centuries and it came to a halt. The computer stopped and put up a red signal, which meant that there was something wrong, either with the information fed into it or with the results compared to the standards. They called in the service department and said, "There is something wrong with the IBM equipment." They checked it and said that it was perfect. The IBM head of operations said, "What's wrong?" They replied, "Well, we have found that there is a day missing in space in elapsed time over the last several thousand years. A day is missing!" You cannot have a missing day in elapsed time, because any scientist knows that the sun does the same thing every day and so does the moon. They scratched their heads and tore their hair. There was no answer!'

The article went on to reveal that the scientist found their missing day in the story in Joshua 10 of the sun standing still and an incident in 2 Kings 20 of the sun moving back ten degrees.

Rainbow of grace

The article was read excitedly by Christians and quoted in sermons to prove that these two amazing Old Testament stories actually happened. Unfortunately the article was a hoax and the magazines that published it had to acknowledge they had been duped. Why were believers so eager to accept the story? Is it that we ourselves are not too sure about some of the remarkable biblical stories? Are we losing our belief in the authority and sufficiency of Scripture? Unless we are careful, our eagerness for scientific backup can bring more discredit upon Scripture than all the abuse and scorn of unbelievers.

Our faith in the story of the ark and the Flood is essentially the same as Noah's. He did not have any physical proof of the coming of the Flood yet he obeyed the commands of God. He did this, says Hebrews 11, 'by faith'. So too our faith has to be in the word of the living God.

The Flood

We can bring the same test of credibility to the Flood as we did to the ark. Scripture makes it clear that the Flood was not limited to one locality but was worldwide. The fact is that many nations have flood stories in their history and these nations are spread all over the world. This has to be significant. The details in these stories vary considerably but the one constant fact is that the world was flooded and only a few people were saved.

Geology cannot prove either way if there was a worldwide flood but it does throw up some interesting facts. Scattered throughout the world are large caches of animal bones and these are usually found on high hilltops. Boice writes that 'Such fissures have been found in England, France, Southern Spain, Germany, Russia, and other countries. The interesting thing about them is that many are filled with bones of such animals as elephants, rhinoceroses, hippopotamuses, reindeer, horses, pigs and oxen. The skeletons are not intact. They have been ripped apart. But the bones are not scattered. They are thrown together in almost unbelievable profusion.'[3] One explanation for these caches could be a great flood of water. It is not conclusive proof but it is a credible explanation.

The flood story in Genesis is not just a quaint story of little or no importance to the Christian faith. The warning of Jesus in Matthew 24:37-41 is that the Flood was a terrible demonstration of the wrath of God. This wrath is all consuming and though the Flood will never be repeated, God's judgement is still to be faced by sinners and none will escape except those who find salvation in Christ. As Noah was safe in the ark so all God's people are safe in Christ. The worldwide Flood is important because it is evidence of a final, universal judgement and as such must be taken seriously.

6.
Noah, a preacher of righteousness

It is impossible for us to understand the intensity of grief that God feels over human sin. The Christian is so familiar with sin, both before and after his conversion, that he can accommodate it. We can tolerate what God cannot and we can excuse what God will not. The more Christlike we become as the sanctifying work of the Holy Spirit takes hold of us, the more difficult this toleration becomes. But even at our best we will never experience the grief that sin brings to the heart of God.

In Genesis 6 man's sin causes the holy God to be sorry (NKJV — 'grieved' in the NIV) that he ever made man and his verdict is that enough is enough. 'My Spirit will not contend with man for ever, for he is mortal; his days will be a hundred and twenty years' (Gen. 6:3). The judgement that the Lord pronounces in verse 7, 'I will wipe mankind, whom I have created, from the face of the earth', is devastating.

But it is perfectly just; the terms of man's existence on earth have been violated and the God who created man can also remove him from the earth. Yet even in this exercise of a legitimate justice, God still offers man mercy and gives him 120 years to consider his ways and repent. God always goes beyond what we might expect and he fixes one last period for the repentance of mankind. But will that 120 years make any difference? We can see now that it did not, but the glory of grace is in the Lord who offers it, not in the sinner who may or may not receive it. God introduced into that 120 years a factor that grace always delights in. Noah began to under-take a ministry to his contemporaries. He was, says the apostle Peter, a preacher of righteousness (2 Peter 2:5).

Light

Noah was a lonely light in an unsympathetic and ungodly society. That is not unlike the situation that many Christians find themselves in today. It is not unusual to be the only Christian in a family, in a class, an office or a factory. Neither is it unusual to be the only Bible believer in a church. If this grieves us, how much more does it hurt the heart of God. But if we believe in the God of providence we know that we are in such situations in order to shine as light into that spiritual and moral darkness. The question has to be, how can we do this in an effective way? It is possible for our Christian witness to merely irritate people as a 'holier-than-thou' attitude emerges. It is also possible to speak in language that is unintelligible to our hearers so that our witness leaves them ignorant of the gospel. And such is the difficulty of the task that we often lose heart and console ourselves with the belief that none will listen, so why bother.

There would have been no point in God giving the people in Genesis 120 years to repent if there was no light of truth shining in the world to point them to repentance. In the same way today the gospel principle remains unaltered: 'How, then, can they call on the one they have not believed in? And how can they believe in the one of whom they have not heard? And how can they hear without someone preaching to them?' (Rom. 10:14). We are the Noahs of our day. This is still a day of grace and God has not yet brought down the curtain on history, so we are to shine as light to point sinners to Jesus. We are to do so, not with a smug superiority, but with the knowledge that we are no better than our hearers and apart from the grace of God we would be under the same judgement as they are. Also, we are to tell them the gospel in words and concepts they can understand, and we are not to lose heart because we know if God can save us he can save anyone.

Noah's light shone out in two ways. Firstly, in the act of building the ark. Everyone else was concerned with the here and now. They were 'eating and drinking, marrying and giving in marriage'. Noah too had to eat and drink and obviously he was concerned about things like marriage, because he himself and his sons got married. But above all of that, he had an eye to the future and to what God had said. His whole life was taken up with the effect of human sin upon the heart of God, and God's response to that sin. By building the ark he showed the unbelieving world that he took God seriously.

Every plank he sawed, every nail he hammered told the world that God was a holy God who would not tolerate their sin. The only reason for the existence of the ark was the reality of man's sin and the reality that God was going to deal with it. As long as Christians today insist upon being preoccupied with the world and taking their standards and attitudes from that world, we are keeping unbelievers from taking God seriously. We are, in fact, urging them to continue in their rebellion and give them no reason to consider the claims of God. Noah's faith condemned the world — does ours? Or does what they see in us merely strengthen their resolve to reject the grace of God? Some Christians are determined not to be so 'heavenly minded that they become no earthly good', but in reality they end up by being so earthly minded that they are no heavenly good. They are not light, but at best a dim flickering non-entity, with nothing to say to the people around them. Noah challenged men and women both with God's righteousness and his own.

Preaching

Noah was a preacher of righteousness, but how did he preach? Did he organize great public gatherings and address the people that way? If people would have come and listened it would have been a good method but it is doubtful if the sort of people described in Genesis 6 would have attended such a meeting. So how did he preach? Was it to informal small groups; to individuals when the opportunity arose? We do not know, but we do know that if preaching is to have any effect at all it must reach the people. There can be no evangelism unless unbelievers are present.

If we do not know what method Noah used, we do know the content of his preaching. He preached righteousness. Centuries later in the New Testament we find the apostles doing exactly the same thing. In the opening chapter of Romans Paul tells us why the gospel is so important: 'For in the gospel a righteousness from God is revealed, a righteousness that is by faith from first to last, just as it is written: "The righteous will live by faith"' (1:17). Dr Lloyd-Jones says that righteousness means a conformity to God, a conformity to God's law, a conformity to God's demands.[1] Righteousness is that which is acceptable to God, which is well pleasing in God's sight; so righteousness in man must mean that he is capable of meeting God's demands. This being the case, man's greatest need is to be righteous, to be acceptable to God but 'there is no one righteous' (Rom. 3:10). So the prime function of the gospel is to provide for the guilty sinner a righteousness. This righteousness comes to us through faith in Christ, 'But now a righteousness from God, apart from law, has been made known, which the Law and the Prophets testify. This righteousness from God comes through faith in Jesus Christ to all who believe' (Rom. 3:21-22).

The people of Noah's day, whose every inclination and thought was only evil all the time, did not need religion or moral exhortation. They were way past that. They needed to find what Noah found — grace in the eyes of the Lord. They needed something done to them and in them of which there was no possible explanation other than that God had done it. Righteousness comes to the sinner after he is first of all brought to see that he has no righteousness of his own that is acceptable to God. The gospel first convicts of sin before it deals with the sin. Sin is dealt with when Jesus is seen as the Righteous One who alone can take away our guilt and condemnation and make us right with God.

So Jesus tells us that the Holy Spirit's ministry is to 'convict the world of guilt in regard to sin and righteousness and judgement' (John 16:8). John Brown says, 'The sin they needed to be convicted of was their own sin; the righteousness they needed to be convicted of was the righteousness of him whom they regarded and treated as an impostor and deceiver; and the judgement they needed to be convicted of was his government — his rightful authority and dominion over them.' [2] Brown then goes on to say, 'The doctrine and the law of Christ cannot be received, except by those who are persuaded that they are sinners, guilty and depraved creatures — exposed to God's righteous displeasure — unfit for God's holy fellowship. The gospel is throughout a restorative economy, and, therefore, can be understood, valued, accepted, only by those who are aware that the lost condition, for which such an economy is required and intended, is theirs.'

We see this being applied by Paul when preaching to Felix in Acts 24. Tacitus, the first century Roman historian, tells us that Felix was a brutal and incompetent politician. Something of this can be seen in verse 26 in his hoping for a bribe from Paul and also in verse 27 in his currying of favour with the Jews. In verse 24 Felix's wife Drusilla is mentioned. This woman was a ravishing beauty whom Felix had seduced from her husband with the help of a magician. To this totally immoral couple Paul preached 'on righteousness, self-control and judgement to come' (v. 25). This ungodly man was afraid as he listened. The Authorized Version says he trembled, but sadly his response was the same as those to whom Noah preached — he refused to heed the warning and the offer of salvation.

At the end of the twentieth century we are confronting a world that is basically the same as Noah's. It is under God's judgement and that judgement will come in God's time, therefore it needs to hear the gospel. The world needs all Christians to be preachers of righteousness. We may never get into a pulpit but every classroom, every place of work, every home is a place to speak of man's lack of righteousness, of his sin and guilt and of the perfect righteousness that he can obtain in Christ. Most people may not listen but still they need to be told. God gave Noah's generation 120 years to repent. How long he is giving ours we do not know, but we do know that the Lord expects us to speak for him to all those around us.

7.
God's covenant with Noah

The concept of covenant is crucial for a biblical understanding of the relationship between God and his people. In the story of Noah the word covenant occurs for the first time (it is found over 270 times in Scripture). But even before this there was the eternal covenant made between God the Father and God the Son. This is sometimes called the covenant of redemption. In this covenant the Father gave to the Son, and the Son undertook to redeem, a people chosen out of all mankind on the sole grounds of God's free grace and mercy. That this predates the covenant with Noah can be seen from passages such as John 17:24, Ephesians 1:4 and 1 Peter 1:20.

Biblical covenants

A covenant is normally a contract between two equal parties, but God's covenants with man cannot come into this category, for who is equal to God? Boice says, 'Basically a covenant is a promise of God to people with whom he is dealing in a special way.'[1] So in the Old Testament we see God's covenants with Noah, Abraham, Moses and David. In the New Testament a covenant is clearly not a mutual agreement between God and man, but a sovereign act of God's free grace. The Lord initiates this covenant and its purpose is always redemptive (see, for example, Heb. 8:6).

The Bible speaks of an old covenant and a new covenant. In the New Testament, the phrase 'old covenant' always refers to the law given through Moses at Mount Sinai — see Hebrews 8:7-13. The old covenant could not save anyone. It provided for human sin, but these provisions were only shadows of the true or symbols of the coming Christ. The law could only point, it could not save.

But what about believers before the time of Christ? Was there no saving covenant for them? Clearly, there must have been, since many of them are held up to us in the New Testament as men of faith whose example we should follow. They did have a saving covenant and it was called the covenant of promise (Gal. 3:15-18). The sacrifices which were commanded under the old covenant all pointed to the sacrifice of Christ on the cross. It was as they pointed to and were fulfilled in Christ that they provided salvation for those Old Testament saints — hence the name covenant of promise, since Christ was the one who was promised (see Heb. 9:1-15; 10:1-10).

Noah

In the covenant with Noah we see all the basic ingredients of God's covenant mercy, and it is apparent that the covenant is not a partnership but rather God making and keeping his promises.

In Genesis 3 we read how sin entered human experience. From then on sin becomes the dominant factor in human nature and in Genesis 4 we see the influence of sin spreading beyond Adam and Eve to their son Cain. Ultimately, in Genesis 5, we read of sin reigning throughout the human race. By the time we arrive at Genesis 6, sin's influence is total, as we have seen in those terrible words in verses 5 and 7.

Noah lay under the wrath and judgement of God, along with the rest of mankind, for he too was a sinner. But this particular sinner was promised salvation, and it is in this that we begin to see the character of the covenant. God knew before time began that man would fall into sin and would be under the threat of his judgement. God's heart prompted him to institute the plan of salvation, the covenant of redemption. According to this plan, he determined to redeem from their sin and lost condition 'a great multitude that no one can count' (Rev. 7:9). Those to be saved he 'chose in [Christ] before the creation of the world, to be holy and blameless in his sight' (Eph. 1:4).

Let us be clear. These chosen ones were not selected for any good that God foresaw in them, but out of God's free, unmerited grace. Noah found grace in the eyes of the Lord, and grace always speaks of the lack of merit on man's part and the abundance of mercy on God's. In effect, Noah did not find grace, but the grace of God found Noah. The initiative, as always, was God's. The fact is that God chose Noah and not that Noah chose God. Noah did not earn grace because he was righteous and blameless, for by definition grace cannot be earned.

Into Noah's meritless situation came salvation which he did not, and could not, ever deserve, nor could he have achieved it by his own efforts. And the reason for this salvation is that God promised him, 'I will establish my covenant with you' (Gen. 6:18). Do you see the situation? On the one hand, God's holiness and hatred of sin set his judgement in action; and on the other, God's mercy and love put his eternal covenant to work. Both are in operation at the same time. Noah was not whisked away magically out of the ravages of the Flood. He had to face that like all men. What the covenant did for Noah was to wrap him around with a God-given protection, namely the ark. This guaranteed him salvation when the waters of divine judgement came upon the earth. The ark was a picture of Christ, bearing the onslaught of the storm and thus protecting those who are 'in him' from judgement.

Genesis 6 ends with a fine testimony to Noah, that he 'did everything just as God commanded him'. This comes after God promised him the blessings of the covenant and as a consequence of that covenant. The covenant is not a covenant of works but a covenant of grace. Obedience is necessary not to make the covenant work, and still less to bring the covenant about, but rather to enjoy its blessings. The only thing that keeps it working is the grace and mercy of God.

8.
The rainbow of grace

In Genesis 6 God establishes his covenant with Noah. The necessity of that covenant for Noah is seen in Genesis 7. Then in chapter 8 the blessing of the covenant is experienced by Noah and his family. But at the end of the chapter God makes a promise: 'Never again will I curse the ground because of man, even though every inclination of his heart is evil from childhood. And never again will I destroy all living creatures, as I have done. As long as the earth endures, seedtime and harvest, cold and heat, summer and winter, day and night will never cease' (Gen. 8:21-22). This promise was crucial for Noah's future peace of mind and well-being. Would God do again to the world what he did in the Flood? He had found grace in the eyes of the Lord but would that grace continue for ever? As well as this he must have feared for his wife and immediate family. He had brothers and sisters that had perished in the Flood and this would have left deep emotional scars in him. Would he or his descendants have to experience this all over again? The promise reassures him concerning this. In chapter 9 God gives a visible sign to the validity of the pledge: '"This is the sign of the covenant I am making between me and you and every living creature with you, a covenant for all generations to come. I have set my rainbow in the clouds, and it will be the sign of the covenant between me and the earth. Whenever I bring clouds over the earth and the rainbow appears in the clouds, I will remember my covenant between me and you and all living creatures of every kind. Never again will the waters become a flood to destroy all life. Whenever the rainbow appears in the clouds, I will see it and remember the everlasting covenant between God and all living creatures of every kind on the earth." So God said to Noah, "This is the sign of the covenant I have established between me and all life on the earth'" (9:12-17).

The rainbow was a sign to Noah of the covenant and a testimony to the eternal value of grace. He could not live in the ark for ever. It only provided a temporary salvation and as soon as Noah left the ark he built an altar and worshipped the Lord. This action revealed the heart of this righteous man. He wanted God in his life and was totally convinced that the blessings of grace are not as valuable as the God of grace.

The reason for the promise

Why did God make this promise? Mankind would not change from the description given in Genesis 6:5. In fact God acknowledges this in the words of the promise: '... even though every inclination of his heart is evil from childhood'. So the promise was not a reward for improved effort on man's part. Neither is the promise an expression of guilt on God's part, as if he had acted too harshly in dealing with man's sin and in the future would be more tolerant of human rebellion. The incident of the tower of Babel in Genesis 11 is an early reminder that God never tolerates sin and always deals with it. The promise says nothing about God's feelings towards sin; it is referring to how God will deal with sin in the future. Calvin makes the point that it is as if God is saying that the restoration of the world was temporary.[1] He had always planned to populate the earth with mankind even though men would continue in their sin. Sin is so dominant in man that if God dealt with us as we deserve there could be a flood every day.

The reason for the promise is tied up in the covenant. It has to do with God's future plans for the world he has created and for men and women made in his image. There is to be a new heaven and earth in which there is no sin, and there are to be sinners born again by the Holy Spirit, men and women remade in the image of Christ. All this would have been beyond the understanding of Noah at that time, but it would have been sufficient for him to understand that in the promise God was guaranteeing mankind a future. Today, with the full and complete revelation of Scripture, we look 'forward to a new heaven and a new earth, the home of righteousness'. The apostle Peter continues: 'So then, dear friends, since you are looking forward to this, make every effort to be found spotless, blameless and at peace with him… Therefore, dear friends, since you already know this, be on your guard so that you may not be carried away by the error of lawless men and fall from your secure position. But grow in the grace and knowledge of our Lord and Saviour Jesus Christ. To him be glory both now and for ever. Amen' (2 Peter 3:13-14, 17-18).

The promise is not an incentive to sin and lawlessness as if God will now turn a blind eye to our faults, but an incentive to holiness.

The nature of the promise

The nature of the promise is to be seen in the abounding grace of God towards guilty sinners. Man's nature since the Fall is polluted by sin and, this side of heaven, he will always be in need of forgiveness. But there are no grounds for forgiveness other than in the unmerited grace of God. Even the need for God to make the promise emphasizes the fact of man's sin and guilt. If we could live faithfully before them, the question of judgement would never arise. Judgement is only necessary because man's sin is a reality. Grace ministers to guilty men and women in their sin. It is not a reward for faithfulness but a gift to the unfaithful. It reflects human need and the love in the heart of God to meet that need. Grace comes from the heart of God that is grieved and pained by human sin. Yet, it is this same offended God who chose a people for himself and redeemed them by paying the price for their sin, by punishing in their place his Son, the Lord Jesus Christ (John 3:16). This is why grace is always amazing and staggering. It originates in the pained heart of God and flows to the guilty heart of man. There is nothing in this world so amazing as divine grace, nothing so breathtaking in its concept, nothing so undeserving and nothing so totally successful in accomplishing its purpose.

A thing of beauty

The sign of grace to Noah was the rainbow set in the clouds. Clouds were a reminder to Noah that it could and would rain again, but the rainbow was the assurance that the rain would never again be an instrument of worldwide judgement. The rainbow itself was a thing of beauty but its true worth was to serve to remind God of his covenant with his people (9:16).

The question has to be asked as to why God needed a sign to remind him of his covenant promise. The answer is that he did not need it. As Derek Kidner says, 'Remember is used in its common meaning, rather than that noted at 8:1; the whole tone of the paragraph is accommodated to our need of simple reassurance.'[2] Here is grace revealing God's deep concern for man's peace of mind. He will never forget but we may, so the rainbow was for Noah's assurance, not for God's memory. There is in us always a tendency to forget or doubt the mercies of God. Perhaps this is understandable because grace is such a staggering concept. We like to trust what we think we have deserved but sin has robbed us of all deserving and without grace we have nothing. The promises of God, particularly in regard to salvation, have to be believed by faith. Once our feelings enter into it we are always floundering.

Salvation is all of grace and depends upon what God has done for us not upon what we may feel at any given moment. The story is told of the Passover night in Egypt. Two boys lived next door to each other and both were the first-born in their families. They knew that life or death for them depended upon the blood sprinkled on the doorposts of their homes.

God had promised that when he saw the blood he would pass over that house and death would not touch it that night. So both watched as their fathers obeyed the word of God and put the blood on the doorposts. That night one boy slept peacefully, confident in the promise of God, whilst next door his friend could not sleep at all. He kept anxiously peeking to see that the blood was still there. The question that arises is, which boy was the safest that night, the one who trusted or the one who worried? The answer is that they were equally as safe as each other. Their salvation did not depend upon their feelings but upon the promise of God that when he saw the blood he would pass over (Exod. 12:13).

That salvation is all of grace is not only a theological necessity but also a truth most beautiful to dwell upon. Like the rainbow, it hovers over us and its beauty thrills our soul. Dr Lloyd-Jones wrote, 'Salvation is not in any sense God's response to anything in us. It is not something that we in any sense deserve or merit. The whole essence of the teaching at this point, and everywhere in all the New Testament, is that we have no sort or kind of right whatsoever to salvation, that the whole glory of salvation is, that though we deserve nothing but punishment and hell and banishment out of the sight of God to all eternity, yet God, of his own love and grace and wondrous mercy, has granted us this salvation. Now that is the entire meaning of this term grace.'[3]

When we do something that merits a reward there is in us a sense of satisfaction and pride. But when we are the recipients of exactly the opposite to what we deserve there is first of all in us a sense of gratitude and humility, then wonder and amazement, then thrill and excitement, and then our souls are overwhelmed with the giver of such love. There is nothing like a biblical understanding of grace to inspire worship in the believer and to cause us to delight in the beauty of Jesus through whom we have received the grace of God.

How can we measure the worth of grace and how can we evaluate the beauty of Jesus? Dr Lloyd-Jones says, 'If you want to measure grace you do so from the highest heaven down to the cross, and beyond that even to the grave, down amongst the dead. This is the way to see the character of the reign of grace. It was grace, the grace that was in his [Christ's] heart, and in the heart of the Godhead, that led him to do all this — eventually to give his very life a ransom for us and for our sins. He laid aside the insignia of that eternal glory, he came down to earth, he endured the contradiction of sinners, and he went to the death of the cross and all that that involved. It is there you see the bounty, the abundance, the munificence of it all. He gave himself upon the death of the cross. So that aspect of grace is seen most gloriously and most brightly in him.'[4]

The beauty of a rainbow compared to the beauty of Christ is but a dull thing. Its lustre soon passes and becomes only a memory whereas the beauty of Christ and his grace is to be savoured every day and all day. It never goes away, never ceases to operate for us and never loses its power and value. It gives an eternal salvation and keeps the redeemed sinner for ever in the presence of God. It is incomparable, unchallengeable and irresistible, and it is ours in and through the Lord Jesus Christ.

9.
Preserving grace

Of all the men who ever lived none knew better than Noah the terrible consequence of sin. He lived through such a judgement as the world had never seen before or since and will not see again until the final judgement. Having lived through this demonstration of the wrath of God one might think that Noah's experience would keep him from sin in the future. But it was not so and Genesis 9:18-23 shows us this righteous man drunken and naked. The lesson for us from this sad incident is not only that any man is capable of sin but that all men do sin — even those declared righteous in the sight of God (Gen. 7:1), those who have found grace in the eyes of the Lord.

Men need grace because they are sinners and through grace they are delivered from hell and judgement, which is the eternal consequence of sin. God in grace provides for them a new ability and enabling of the Holy Spirit to overcome sin but it does not make them sinless. In fact for the believer sin often becomes more of a problem after salvation than it was before! Because he is aware of the holy God, every temptation becomes a struggle (Rom. 7:9-11). Whereas before he simply yielded to the temptation, now each temptation becomes more intense (Rom. 7:24). How much more does he throw himself upon the promise of Scripture that 'No temptation has seized you except what is common to man. And God is faithful; he will not let you be tempted beyond what you can bear. But when you are tempted, he will also provide a way out so that you can stand up under it' (1 Cor. 10:13). Our problem is that we do not always take the way out but, like Noah, fall into sin, whether the sin be drunkenness, or the sins of adultery, envy, pride etc.

When the believer sins, what use is grace to him? Has he put himself outside the blessings of grace? Has he lost his salvation? Noah's sin, though it grieved and pained the heart of God as all sin does, did not put him outside of grace as the testimony of the New Testament clearly shows us.

The sin of righteous men

If we are to ask the question, why do righteous men sin? — the simple answer is, because they are not sinless. No one in this world is free from the influence of sin and the Bible continually demonstrates this truth by showing us the sin of its great heroes. Abraham was called the friend of God but his life is far from blameless. Moses was a remarkable man and the testimony to him in Hebrews 11 is glowing, but he was not allowed by God to enter the promised land because of his sin. David is described in Scripture as a man after God's own heart, but Scripture also shows us David's moral failures.

Why do outstanding spiritual leaders like these and others sin? Consider, for instance, David and his adultery with Bathsheba. How is it possible for such a man to allow that sin to develop and mature in his life? We acknowledge that no believer is perfect and that we all sin, but this was no flash of temper or moment of selfishness. This was deliberate adultery that led to scheming murder. And David was no inexperienced youngster but a mature man about fifty years old.

David's problem started in 2 Samuel 11:1-2 with what appears to be a casual happening: 'In the spring, at the time when kings go off to war ... David remained in Jerusalem. One evening David got up from his bed and walked around on the roof of the palace. From the roof he saw a woman bathing. The woman was very beautiful.' He did not go looking for trouble, it appeared just to happen. But that is not so. There are two important points here: this man of God was in the wrong place and in the wrong frame of mind. Nothing happens in a Christian's life by accident. We believe in the providence of God that leads and guides us, but if we turn our eyes from the God of providence then we make ourselves prey for the devil's schemes. At other times David may have seen Bathsheba bathing and turned his eyes away. He knew, and would have wholeheartedly agreed with, the words of Job 31:1 to make a covenant with his eyes not to look lustfully at a woman. But now in the wrong place and the wrong frame of mind he ignores all he knows to be right.

David was in the wrong place because he had rejected

the path of duty. He should have been on the battlefield with his soldiers. He was in the wrong frame of mind because he preferred the luxuries of the palace to the hardship of the battlefield. Matthew Henry comments, 'When we are out of the way of our duty, we are in temptation.' This is all very relevant to every believer. None of us are so spiritually strong and so experienced in the Christian life that we become immune to temptation and sin.

Consider this particular sin of adultery. We may think this could never happen to us. But it has happened to a frightening number of evangelical pastors and believers in recent years. The moral climate of the day encourages it. What David saw from his palace roof — a beautiful woman undressing — you could see every day on the television, in the comfort of your home!

How do you deal with these things? You must keep yourself in the battle with all the armour of God on. You must make sure that your mind is spiritually alert and not dozing in moral laziness. Perhaps this was something of Noah's problem. After the pressures of the Flood he was relaxing with a pleasant drink and had gradually allowed this to deteriorate into drunkenness. Sin in a righteous man is a particular grief to God. In condemning his sin, twice David was told that he was guilty of despising the Lord (2 Sam. 12:9-10). There is a sense in which we can say that sin in a believer is far worse than sin in the unbeliever. The unbeliever sins against the law of God. We also sin against that law but we sin too against the light that the Lord has given us and against the love that he has shown us.

Preserving grace

A grace that saved us but did not preserve and keep us would not be of much use, because we all still sin. In fact a grace that saved but did not preserve would not be grace at all. By definition, grace is unmerited by us. It was unmerited when it saved us first of all and it continues to be unmerited after we are saved, as our sin so clearly demonstrates. If grace were something the sinner earned it would be difficult to see why Noah was in the ark and not drowned in the Flood. And if we could somehow explain that, it would be impossible to understand how he could continue to be acceptable to the holy God after his drunken debauchery. The only explanation for Noah and us is to be found in the nature of grace.

Grace can preserve as well as save us because it deals essentially with our standing before God. The heart of the biblical teaching on grace is the justifying work of God in which God credits to the guilty sinner the righteousness of Christ. It is this righteousness that makes us acceptable to God. Nothing else could do this. In Romans Paul spells out certain basic truths about this righteousness.

> It is not earned by us: it is apart from the law
> (Rom. 3:21).
> It is the heart of the gospel (Rom. 1:16-17).
> It is a revealed truth that God must show us if we
> are to understand it and delight in it (Rom. 1:17).
> It is received by faith in Jesus Christ (Rom. 3:22).
> It is what justification gives us (Rom. 3:24).
> It is purchased for us by the atoning death of
> Christ (Rom. 3:25).

Justification is a sovereign work of God. We contribute nothing to it. It is a declaration of God as to how he now regards us — just in his sight, all our sins covered by the blood of Christ. Therefore there are no degrees of justification. Each believer is as justified at the moment of regeneration as he is ever going to be, and no believer is more or less justified than any other Christian. Justification credits to us the righteousness of Jesus and the merits of his atoning death on the cross, which dealt with the root problem of our sin and therefore with all individual sins, past, present and future. So when we sin as Christians, we do not lose our salvation and we do not fall from grace. The grace which saved us goes on working for us and applying to us the cleansing power of the blood of Jesus. Noah's drunkenness, David's adultery, our pride and jealousy, are all dealt with by preserving grace (1 Cor. 1:8; Jude 24).

Most Christians who lose their assurance do so because they have never understood justification. Commenting on Romans 3:24 Dr Lloyd-Jones says of justification, 'It does not mean that we are made righteous, but rather that God regards us as righteous and declares us to be righteous. This has often been a difficulty to many people. They say that because they are conscious of sin within they can not be in a justified state; but anyone who speaks like that shows immediately that he has no understanding of this great and crucial doctrine of justification. Justification makes no actual change in us; it is a declaration by God concerning us. It is not something that results from what we do but rather something that is done to us. We have only been made righteous in the sense that God regards us as righteous, and pronounces us to be righteous.' [1]

If we allow our assurance of salvation to depend upon our actions or our feelings then we are denying that grace is the free, undeserved gift of God. Once we grasp the heart of justification that salvation depends totally upon what God has done for us in Christ then the question of losing our salvation never arises.

Grace preserves and keeps us because it is God who gives the grace. He can do no other than to preserve those whom he has saved. Our salvation cost him his Son; he will therefore preserve us (Rom. 8:32; John 10:28-29). This does not mean that the Christian should be unconcerned about his sin. Sin can rob us of the joy of salvation and the awareness of our peace with God but it cannot take away what God has pronounced to be eternally true of us. More than that, our sin deeply grieves God and this should be something we want to avoid at all cost. Because we are Christians, we love the Christ who died for us. Out of love and gratitude towards him, we constantly strive to become more and more like him. This process of sanctification should be something that we earnestly seek.

10.
Sanctifying grace

The God of grace who saves us also wants us to enjoy the Christian life. Sin will always rob us of that pleasure. Therefore grace works in a sanctifying way in the Christian to overcome the pull of sin. The rainbow of grace was the sign of the covenant that God made with his people. Obedience to the word of God is not essential to the validity of the covenant, as if it depended upon man. If it was it would not have lasted five minutes. But obedience by us is essential if we are to enjoy the blessing of the covenant promises. So sin has to be faced head on and through grace God gives us the power to do this. Paul tells Titus, 'The grace of God that brings salvation has appeared to all men. It teaches us to say, "No" to ungodliness and worldly passions, and to live self-controlled, upright and godly lives in this present age' (Titus 2:11-12).

Natural background

Titus was pastor of the church on Crete and he had a very difficult job. He was ministering to people who were by nature liars, evil brutes and lazy gluttons (1:12). This was the natural background of the converts who made up the church on Crete. So Paul rebukes them so that they may learn to be sound in the faith (1:13). But rebuke is a negative emphasis and therefore more is needed. This he does in chapter 2 of Titus, giving instruction to teach the old men, the old women, the young women, the young men and the slaves.

The grace of God which brings salvation has appeared to all these people, to these liars, evil brutes and lazy gluttons. They have been saved and are now members of the church. Saving grace is able to deal with men and women of all groups and social backgrounds. It can do so because it is God's grace, his unmerited favour to an undeserving people. Grace saved Noah and could well have saved others of his time. It does not matter where grace finds the sinner, the depth of sin is no barrier to salvation. People may be guilty of sins that society regards as acceptable, or of vile offences that make even harden sinners cringe, but the grace of God can deal with all sin.

A pathetic drug addict who drifts through life on lies, cheating and stealing in order to finance his self-destruction has as much hope of salvation as a moral and respectable pillar of society. This is because salvation is all of grace. No matter what a man is, his only hope of salvation is Jesus (Acts 4:12). Spiritually speaking the gospel finds all men and women in exactly the same condition — in this world without God and

without hope. Morally speaking there was no difference between Noah and the rest of the world of his time. There may
have been a difference of degree in the measure of their sin
but they were all sinners (Rom. 3:23). But spiritually speaking, the immense difference existed because Noah found grace
in the eyes of the Lord.

Grace at work

Saving grace not only saves, it also sanctifies. It teaches us to
say 'No' to sin. Saving grace includes sanctifying grace. They
are not two separate things that come to us at different times.
One flows inevitably and instantly out of the other. We can
see this in verse 14 of Titus chapter 2. Why did God redeem
us? In order to purify us and make us eager to do what is
good.

In other words, the evidence that a person is saved is that
he is learning to say no to sin in his life. The evidence that
these liars, evil brutes and lazy gluttons were saved, was that
they were no longer liars, evil brutes and lazy gluttons! The
evidence is not sinlessness, as is clear from Noah's drunkenness. The Bible nowhere teaches sinless perfection this side
of heaven. Saving and preserving grace cover each sin, but
God wants us to overcome the temptation to such sin. He
wants us to say no to it and sanctifying grace teaches us this
as different desires, appetites and ambitions begin to emerge
in our lives.

Do you know what metamorphosis means? It is when a
rather ugly, creepy crawly caterpillar spins a hard cocoon

around itself and some days later emerges as a beautiful butterfly. That is metamorphosis and it is exactly the same word that Paul uses in 2 Corinthians 3:18: 'And we, who with unveiled faces all reflect the Lord's glory, are being transformed [*metamorphoomai* is the Greek word] into his likeness.' Jerry Bridges says, 'I find it somewhat fascinating and instructive that Paul uses the same word that describes the transformation of a caterpillar into a butterfly to describe the spiritual transformation in the life of a Christian.'[1] The process is just as mysterious, and the results are even more striking. Actually the process of transformation that Paul describes very briefly in 2 Corinthians 3:18 is called sanctification.

Grace teaching

Bridges goes on to say that 'Sanctification is the work of the Holy Spirit in us whereby our inner being is progressively changed, freeing us more and more from sinful traits and developing within us over time the virtues of Christlike character.' However, though sanctification is the work of the Holy Spirit in us, it does involve our wholehearted response in obedience and the regular use of the spiritual disciplines that are instruments of sanctification.

The grace that saves also sanctifies, but there is a difference. Saving grace is all of God and what it does, it does instantly, completely and for ever. This is what the Bible calls justification. Sanctifying grace works more slowly because it involves the progressive growth of the saved sinner. It works not by doing it all for us but by teaching us self-discipline. To say no to sin is an act of self-discipline, but it is not merely a matter of will-power but of grace teaching us to hate sin and love righteousness. So as well as the negative of saying 'No', there is the positive emphasis of living self-controlled, upright and godly lives. Or as Paul puts it in another context, it is to put off the old man and put on the new man (Eph. 4:22-24).

It is the same with faith. Faith basically means to believe and trust God — it is the spiritual eyesight of the soul. This is why it comes to us by hearing the Word of God. If there is no word there can be no faith. This is because of what faith is. It is not a step in the dark but a hearing what God has to say, believing it and then acting upon it. Take for instance a man who is not a Christian. He hears God through his Word telling him that he personally is a sinner. It may be that no one else is saying this and perhaps people are saying what a good fellow he is. But the Word of God says he is a sinner. He believes God. He is convicted by the Holy Spirit and looks for an answer. The Holy Spirit shows him the answer in the gospel, he is to repent of his sin and believe in Jesus. So he comes in faith and repentance to Jesus and is saved. It is all by faith. It is not in anything that he does (Eph. 2:8-9). He has contributed nothing to his salvation and is saved by grace through faith. When he is a Christian, he still lives by faith. He believes God as to how he is to live and behave, only now his faith produces action. This is the very evidence of godliness seen in the lives of the great men of God presented in Hebrews 11.

Noah in his drunken state was allowing sin to control his life. He said 'Yes', instead of 'No'. In so doing he dishonoured God and put his sons in a very difficult and embarrassing situation.

When we are being taught it takes time to learn and some learn quicker than others. In the spiritual realm this has nothing to do with intellect and everything to do with desire. Jesus promises that if there is in us a hunger and thirst (intense desire) for righteousness we shall have it (Matt. 5:6). A passing desire to be better Christians, to be more prayerful and more knowledgeable of Scripture simply will not do. This is not the same as hungering and thirsting. If we really want to be more prayerful we must give more time to pray. If we really want our Bible knowledge to increase then we must give more time to Bible study. These things do not just happen, they have to be worked at. They take effort. Grace will give us the desire for them but we must discipline ourselves to achieve the objective. As we strive for these things, so God himself will help us (Col. 1:29).

Noah could have avoided the drunken episode by following the dictates of grace in his heart. The evidence of grace in a life is more grace — the grace that never stops learning and is always seeking to teach us, sometimes by direct command, sometimes by a guilty conscience, but it never stops working.

'For it is by grace you have been saved, through faith — and this not from yourselves, it is the gift of God — not by works, so that no one can boast. For we are God's workmanship, created in Christ Jesus to do good works, which God prepared in advance for us to do' (Eph. 2:8-10).

Notes

Chapter 1

1. John MacArthur, *Drawing Near,* Crossway 1993, reading for 13 November.
2. A. W. Pink, *The Attributes of God,* Guardian Press, 1975, back cover.
3. E. J. Young, *Genesis 3,* Banner of Truth, 1966, pp.113-14.

Chapter 2

1. D. Martyn Lloyd-Jones, *Assurance,* Banner of Truth, 1971, pp.218-19.
2. James Montgomery Boice, *Genesis,* Zondervan, 1982, pp.251-52.

Chapter 3

1. Leupold, *Genesis,* Evangelical Press, 1972, pp.245-6.
2. Boice, *Genesis,* p.255.
3. As above, p.256.

Chapter 4

1. A. W. Pink, *Hebrews,* Baker, 1954, p.680.
2. Gordon Keddie, *Triumph of the King,* Evangelical Press, 1990, p.45.

Chapter 5

1. Whitcomb, *The Early Earth,* Evangelical Press, 1972, p.83.
2. Whiston's *Josephus,* The Excelsior Edition, p.29.
3. Boice, *Genesis*, p.292.

Chapter 6

1. D. Martyn Lloyd-Jones, *The Gospel of God,* Banner of Truth, 1985, p.299.
2. John Brown, *Discourses,* Banner of Truth, 1967, vol. 3, pp.414-16.

Chapter 7
1. Boice, *Genesis,* p.267.

Chapter 8
1. Calvin, *Commentary on Genesis*, Baker, 1979, pp.283-4.
2. Derek Kidner, *Genesis*, Tyndale Press, 1967, p.102.
3. D. Martyn Lloyd-Jones, *God's Way of Reconciliation,* Evangelical Press, 1972, p.130.
4. Lloyd-Jones, *Assurance*, pp.364-5.

Chapter 9
1. D. Martyn Lloyd-Jones, *Atonement and Justification,* Banner of Truth, 1970, p.55.

Chapter 10
1. Jerry Bridges, *The Discipline of Grace,* Navpress, 1994, p.94.